THE ANCIENT WORLD

THE
INCAS

Chloë Sayer

RSVP
RAINTREE
STECK-VAUGHN
PUBLISHERS
A Steck-Vaughn Company

Austin, Texas

THE ANCIENT WORLD

The AZTECS · GREAT AFRICAN KINGDOMS · EGYPT · GREECE · The INCAS · ROME

Published by Raintree Steck-Vaughn Publishers,
an imprint of Steck-Vaughn Company

Library of Congress Cataloging-in-Publication Data
Sayer, Chloë.
The incas / Chloë Sayer.
p.   cm.—(The ancient world)
Includes bibliographical references and index.
Summary: Describes the politics, society, ideas, religion, art, science, entertainment, rural life, and legacy of one of the greatest planned societies the world has ever known.
ISBN 0-8172-5125-1
1. Incas—Juvenile literature.
[1. Incas. 2. Indians of South America.]
I. Title. II. Series: Ancient world.
F3429.S284 1998
985'.019—dc21   97-49247

Printed in Italy. Bound in the United States.
1 2 3 4 5 6 7 8 9 0 03 02 01 00 99

Cover pictures: Inca man with panpipes (left), and textile border with oculate hummingbirds

Picture acknowledgments: Ronald Sheridan, Ancient Art and Architecture Collection Ltd 10 (Mike Andrews), 13, 35, 42 top, 52–3; AKG Photo Library 20 (British Library); C.M.Dixon Cover left, 39 top, 42 middle; David Lavendar 53 bottom; N.J. Saunders 44 inset, 44–5 main; South American Pictures 5 top (Tony Morrison), 5 bottom (Tony Morrison), 6 (Kathy Jarvis), 7 (Kimball Morrison), 9 (Tony Morrison), 12 (Kimball Morrison), 17 (Tony Morrison), 19 (Tony Morrison), 21 (Tony Morrison), 22 (Tony Morrison), 23 (Tony Morrison), 25 (Tony Morrison), 26 (Tony Morrison), 29 (Tony Morrison), 32–3 (Tony Morrison), 32 bottom (Tony Morrison), 34 (Tony Morrison), 36 (Tony Morrison), 37 (Tony Morrison), 43 (Tony Morrison), 46 (Tony Morrison), 48 (Tony Morrison), 49 (Robert Francis), 54–5 (Tony Morrison), 55 inset (Tony Morrison), 56 (Tony Morrison), 57 (Tony Morrison), 58 (Tony Morrison), 59 (Peter Riley), 60 (Tony Morrison); Werner Forman Archive cover right, 1, 8 top (David Bernstein Fine Art, New York), 11 (British Museum, London), 15 (Nick Saunders and Barbara Heller), 18 (Schindler Collection, New York), 24 (Museum fur Volkerkunde, Berlin), 27 (Museum fur Volkerkunde, Berlin), 28 (Museum fur Volkerkunde, Berlin), 30 (Museum fur Volkerkunde, Berlin), 31 (British Museum, London), 38–9 (Museum fur Volkerkunde, Berlin), 40 (Museum fur Volkerkunde, Berlin), 41 (private collection, New York), 47 (Museum fur Volkerkunde, Berlin), 50 (Museum of the American Indian). Map artwork: Peter Bull

Contents

CHAPTER 1

The Inca World

Land of the Four Quarters

The Incas developed one of the greatest planned societies that the world has known. They called their vast empire Tahuantinsuyu, or "Land of the Four Quarters." At its height, in A.D. 1532, Inca civilization stretched more than 3,400 mi. (5,500 km) along South America. The city named Cuzco, which means "navel," lay at the center of Tahuantinsuyu. From their imperial capital, Inca rulers governed the lands that are now Peru, western Bolivia, Ecuador, northern Chile, upland Argentina, and the south of Colombia. To unite this immense area, the Incas had to overcome the difficulties of a hostile environment.

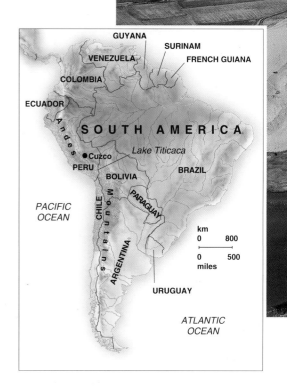

Desert, Mountains, and Jungles

Inca territories included very different landscapes and climates. Bordering the Pacific Ocean, like a narrow ribbon, lies the world's driest coastal desert. Rain seldom falls on this wasteland. Among the sand dunes, however, are a number of fertile valleys; these are watered by seasonal streams from the mountains behind. People who lived along the coast in ancient times understood the preservative qualities of the desert. They buried works of art with their dead; these have been protected from decay over many hundreds of years by the barren sands.

▲ This map shows the South American continent, and Tahuantinsuyu, the vast region governed by the Incas (shaded pink). Between coastal desert in the west and dense jungle in the east rise the Andes. Cuzco, the Inca capital, is located in the highlands of present-day Peru.

◀ The western edge of South America contains the world's driest coastal desert. The green fields seen here are irrigated with water from the Ocana River as it flows into the Pacific Ocean.

▼ For the Incas and their predecessors, the Amazonian rain forest was a source of exotic animals, brilliant feathers, plant fibers, and dyes. Seen here is a scarlet macaw with richly colored plumage.

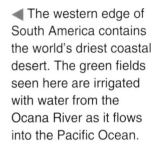

The Andes form the world's longest mountain chain and rise to an altitude of 22,800 ft. (6,960 m). There, temperatures soar during the day and plunge at night. Glaciers fill the highest valleys, and several rivers cross the Andes. Lake Titicaca, the highest major body of water on Earth, lies between Peru and Bolivia. Farming is possible on parts of the high plateau and in deep valley basins. Summer, from December to March, is the rainy season in the highlands. To the east of the Andes stretches the dense rain forest of the Amazon River basin.

CHAPTER 2

Before the Incas

The First Settlers

The Central Andes have been inhabited by humans for more than 12,000 years. Gradually hunters and plant-gatherers learned how to domesticate animals and to cultivate food crops. Intensive farming, which spread slowly across the Central Andes from about 1800 B.C., allowed settlers to improve the quality of their lives and to colonize new habitats. The presence at Chiripa, on the southern side of Lake Titicaca, of weaving tools, decorated pottery, and ceramic trumpets, together with the evidence of basic architectural skills, marked a great advance in the history of this area.

The Cult of Chavín

The Incas were preceded by a long line of important South American civilizations. The town of Chavín de Huántar, in the Peruvian Andes, became a center for art and religion. This distinctive culture, called Chavín by archaeologists, lasted from approximately 900 B.C. to 200 B.C. Religious beliefs and practices were highly organized. An imposing temple, built by expert stone-masons, faced the rising sun and became a center of pilgrimage. Chavín culture influenced art and architecture all over northern Peru.

▲ Elaborate stone carvings decorated many of the buildings at Chavín de Huántar. They reflected a cult whose gods were mythological men and beasts. This head is one of many: together they show different stages in the transformation of a shaman into a monstrous animal spirit.

Tiahuanaco

The damp climate of the high valleys has destroyed the remains left by many Andean peoples. Chavín culture is known to us only because some of its ceramics and stonework have survived. This is also true of the much later culture at Tiahuanaco, near Lake Titicaca. On a desolate plain in Bolivia, 12,600 ft. (3,840 m) above sea level, an imposing temple city flourished between A.D. 100 and A.D. 1250. At its peak, Tiahuanaco had more than 20,000 inhabitants. Massive blocks of stone, shaped so that they fitted together perfectly, formed grand monuments, buildings, and other structures. Trade links with the Amazon rain forest and the Pacific coast enabled the people of Tiahuanaco to export potatoes and other highland produce. In return they obtained corn, cotton, tropical fruits, and metals. Over time the influence of Tiahuanaco spread down to the coast. Whether through drought, earthquake, or revolt, this once great capital was then abandoned and left to decay.

▲ The Gateway of the Sun at Tiahuanaco, in the Andes of Bolivia, reaches a height of 10 ft. (3.04 m), and was carved from a single block of stone. Above the entrance the figure of a god holds a spear-thrower. He is surrounded by winged attendants with bird and human heads.

During the Great Ice Age, low sea levels exposed a wide platform of land between Siberia and the western coast of Alaska. This was the route taken after 30,000 B.C. by nomadic tribes from Asia. As they gradually fanned out across North, Central, and South America, distinct cultures developed without any known outside influence until the arrival of Europeans approximately 500 years ago.

The Paracas Burials

While Chavín culture was developing in the highlands, coastal groups were also developing. The people of Paracas reached new technical and artistic heights. Dating from around 600 B.C., Paracas culture takes its name from a peninsula on the south coast of Peru. Sited there were two burial grounds. Wrapped in textiles, more than 500 crouched bodies have been preserved in the the desert for about 2,500 years.

The oldest cemetery, known as Paracas Cavernas, consists of deep, underground chambers. Gifts of clothing, gourds, and thin gold ornaments accompanied the dead on their journey beyond the grave. Also present were magnificent examples of colorfully decorated pottery. The designs show Chavín influence. The skulls of the dead had been deformed in childhood: tight bindings may have been used to artificially flatten heads, perhaps regarded as a sign of beauty.

The cemetery known as Paracas Necropolis was at ground level. The dead were placed in baskets in a sitting position, wrapped in cloth, and buried in the sand with weapons, gold ornaments, feather fans, animals, pottery, and gourds. They were given food to sustain them in the afterlife. Finely embroidered clothing, woven from cotton or wool, makes this one of the richest textile finds anywhere in the world. Designs include mythological creatures, animals, and geometric patterns.

The Nazca Lines

The Nazca Valley, on the south coast of Peru, has given its name to the civilization that flourished there after 200 B.C.

▲ This richly embroidered Paracas textile shows a supernatural being in human form. His legs are flanked by two birds, and a snakelike creature hovers above his head.

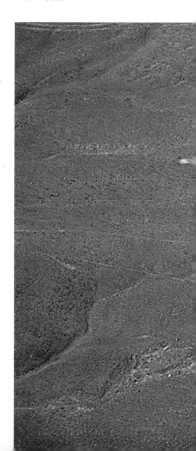

Influenced by Paracas culture, the people of Nazca created pottery and textiles decorated with bird, animal, and fish designs. They are best remembered for the vast figures that they drew across the arid landscape. Known as the Nazca lines, these take the form of abstract shapes, animals, and birds. Some of the lines are very long. One bird measures 400 ft. by 300 ft. (122 m by 91.5 m). To make the lines, shallow furrows were cut through the surface of the desert, exposing the lighter soil beneath. We do not know what purpose the lines fulfilled.

Nazca people lived in adobe houses clustered in villages. They built small pyramids, but no great forts or temples. Their crops were irrigated with water brought by aqueducts from the mountains. In the seventh century A.D., the Nazca were conquered by the warlike Huari. For a time, Huari civilization flourished. Then, in approximately A.D. 800, the Huari capital was abandoned.

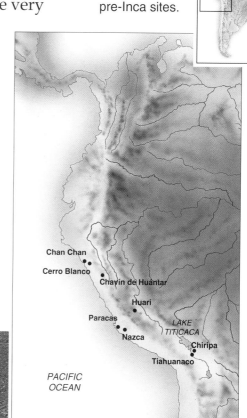

▼ This map shows some of the chief pre-Inca sites.

◄ Nazca culture flourished on the arid coastal plain of southern Peru. Mystery surrounds the famous Nazca lines. Shown here is a hummingbird. Such designs can only be appreciated fully when viewed from the sky— something the ancient Nazca were unable to do.

Moche Culture

Moche (or Mochica) culture originated during the first century A.D. in the Moche and Chicama valleys on the north coast of Peru. From their administrative capital, the warlike Moche conquered and unified weaker groups, establishing the first state or kingdom of the Andes. Giant temple platforms and buildings were made of adobe bricks. At Cerro Blanco, the pyramid known as Huaca del Sol (Pyramid of the Sun) stood over 135 ft. (41 m) tall. The Moche also built earthen aqueducts to irrigate their fields. Where steep slopes made farming difficult, they constructed terraces to increase the amount of fertile land available. Although we know little about the Moche, it is clear that theirs was a well-organized society. Priests and elite warriors belonged to the ruling class, and farmers and craftworkers supported the state with their labor.

▼ Chan Chan was the largest city ever built in ancient Peru. Today it looks like a mud ruin in the desert, but it was once a flourishing and well-planned city. Its streets ran at right angles, and its houses were neatly positioned.

The Chimú

The culture of the Moche eventually died out, and was replaced after A.D. 900 by that of the Chimú. This race of warriors built up a large empire, known as Chimor, along 620 mi. (1,000 km) of Pacific coastland. A network of roads linked Chimú settlements. The capital, Chan Chan, was built of sun-dried mud bricks. It covered a vast area and held about 50,000 people. Water was brought into the city and stored in reservoirs to irrigate fields and gardens. Several thousand state-supported craftspeople lived in Chan Chan, including weavers, woodworkers, and metalsmiths. The Moche had known how to cast gold, how to solder it, and how to alloy it with silver and copper. Chimú metalsmiths improved on Moche techniques. They created magnificent collars of round beads, beaten face masks, crowns, and breastplates. Chimú civilization was still flourishing when the Incas began their rise to power.

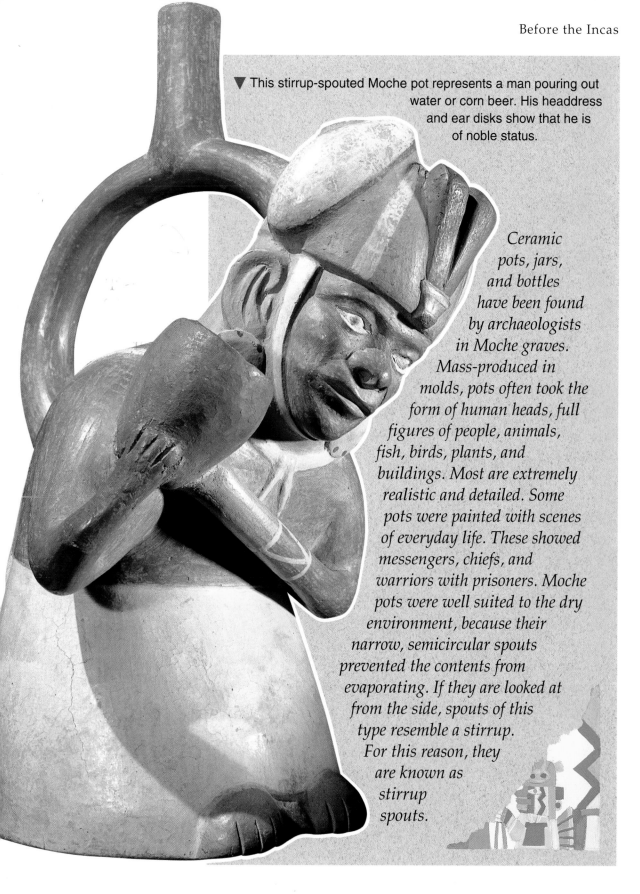

▼ This stirrup-spouted Moche pot represents a man pouring out water or corn beer. His headdress and ear disks show that he is of noble status.

Ceramic pots, jars, and bottles have been found by archaeologists in Moche graves. Mass-produced in molds, pots often took the form of human heads, full figures of people, animals, fish, birds, plants, and buildings. Most are extremely realistic and detailed. Some pots were painted with scenes of everyday life. These showed messengers, chiefs, and warriors with prisoners. Moche pots were well suited to the dry environment, because their narrow, semicircular spouts prevented the contents from evaporating. If they are looked at from the side, spouts of this type resemble a stirrup. For this reason, they are known as stirrup spouts.

CHAPTER 3

The Inca Story

▼ The Andes are the second-highest mountain chain on Earth. They stretch for more than 4,200 mi. (6,740 km). Shown here are the snow-covered peaks of Mount Hayna Potosí in Bolivia.

Legendary Beginnings

Mystery surrounds the early history of the Incas, who had no written records of their past. According to legend, the Inca dynasty was founded by Manco Capac, son of the Sun. Manco Capac first appeared from a cave in southern Peru with his sister-wife Mama Ocllo, daughter of the Moon. Other close relatives followed, along with the people of ten ayllus (clans). All these people were looking for fertile land.

The Sun gave Manco Capac a golden rod, and said: "If you plunge this rod into the ground and it disappears, you will know that you have found the predestined place where you must build your city." Manco Capac looked among the mountains for a suitable site—one where the soil was deep enough for agriculture. During this journey he murdered his brothers and became chief. The rod disappeared into the ground at Cuzco. Manco Capac and Mama Ocllo settled, won over the local tribes, and established their capital.

Later, the spot where the earth had swallowed up the golden rod was marked by a great temple in honor of the Sun.

Manco Capac, the first Inca ruler of Cuzco, was, in reality, probably the chieftain of a tribe from the highlands. In the Quechua language, the word "Inca" means chief. Under the leadership of Manco Capac, from about A.D. 1200, the Incas crushed local resistance and began to strengthen their position in the region.

The Incas prided themselves on having taught local inhabitants the arts of weaving, agriculture, and herding. But, because they arrived late on the historical scene, the reverse was true; the Incas had benefited from the cultural advances made by earlier peoples. The genius of the Incas lay in their dedication. They were brilliant organizers and disciplined warriors. From these small beginnings, the Inca empire would spread to its greatest size in just 300 years.

Because Inca legends stressed the divine nature of Inca ancestry, they played a crucial role in the Inca's rise to power. They showed that the founding of their capital at Cuzco, and the eventual creation of their mighty empire, had been the will of Inti, the Sun God.

▲ This portrait of Manco Capac, legendary founder of the Inca royal family, was created from the imagination by Felipe Guamán Poma de Ayala in the sixteenth century. The word "Inca," which means chief, was originally used by Manco Capac.

The Incas were ideally suited to their hostile environment. Like most Peruvian highlanders, they were not very tall, on the average 5.2 ft. (1.6 m). Physically strong and capable of enduring great hardship, they had broad shoulders and the deep chests characteristic of people who live in the thin atmosphere of the High Andes. They had copper-colored skin, broad faces with prominent noses, and almost no facial hair.

The Rise to Power

For approximately 200 years after settling at Cuzco, the Incas devoted their energies to plundering raids and minor wars with neighboring tribes. Manco Capac was succeeded by six rulers who defended the small mountain state around Cuzco, but failed to extend their powers farther. The reign of Viracocha Inca, the eighth ruler, ended with a military threat from the north. It was posed by the Chanca. Menacing and increasingly powerful, the Chanca defeated the Quechua, whose territories adjoined those of the Incas. They then advanced on Cuzco. Viracocha Inca—old and weak—withdrew. The situation was saved by his son, Yupanqui, who called upon his followers and defeated the invading army. With the Chanca subdued, the Incas found themselves supreme in the highlands.

In 1438 Yupanqui was proclaimed emperor under the name of Pachacuti (World Reverser). New alliances were formed. Widely regarded as the true founder of the Inca empire, Pachacuti united neighboring populations and made loyal Quechua subjects honorary Inca citizens. They were known as "Incas by privilege." Pachacuti also began a long series of aggressive foreign wars. In the south, the Incas conquered the Lupaca, the Colla, and other kingdoms around Lake Titicaca. The coastal Chimú kingdom was conquered around 1470. With each victory, the army grew larger and more experienced.

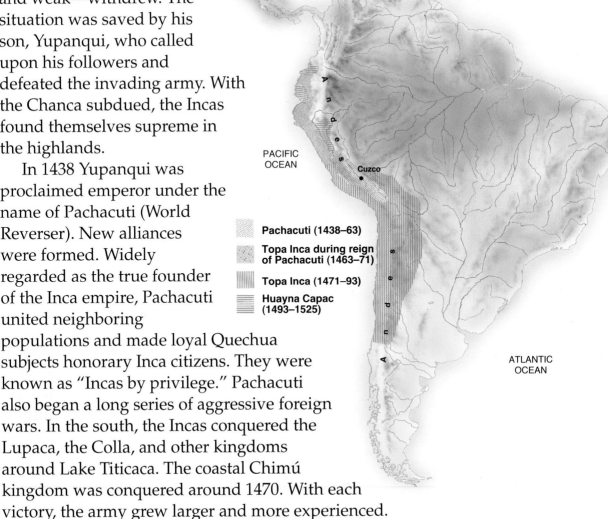

▼ This map charts the growth of the Inca empire. Different colors show the territories conquered by successive emperors. Victory over the pink areas is generally attributed to Topa Inca during his father's reign. Because events were reported orally by the Incas, the dates can only be regarded as approximate.

PACIFIC OCEAN

Cuzco

Pachacuti (1438–63)

Topa Inca during reign of Pachacuti (1463–71)

Topa Inca (1471–93)

Huayna Capac (1493–1525)

ATLANTIC OCEAN

ELSETÍMO CAPÍTÃ INGA·MAITAC·

▲ Resistance to Inca expansion was often from hilltop forts. Protected by walls and moats, armies hoped to withstand the attack. The Incas won many battles by subjecting their enemies to long sieges.

At Pachacuti's death in 1471, power passed to his son, Topa Inca. A gifted commander, Topa Inca had already led many military campaigns. Now he expanded the empire along more than 2,500 mi. (4,000 km) of frontier, from central Ecuador to central Chile. Policies for the administration of newly acquired provinces were improved during his reign. Topa Inca was followed in 1493 by Huayna Capac. The eleventh emperor, Huayna Capac strengthened the Inca's position and added some new territories. Before he died in 1525, Ecuador had been fully integrated into the Inca empire.

Military Might

The creation of Tahuantinsuyu ("Land of the Four Quarters") demanded military skills. Strategy played an important role. Often the Inca army divided itself into three: while one force engaged the enemy in battle, the other two would stage a surprise attack from the rear. Sometimes the enemy took refuge in a hilltop fortress; the Incas then cut off their supply of food and water. Once defeated, enemy soldiers were allowed to return home as Inca subjects.

As Inca armies grew in size, enlarged by the flow of conscripts from newly conquered provinces, they came to rely on a range of weapons. Fighting was usually started at long range by slingers; then arrows were fired by bowmen. Clubs and spears were deployed in hand-to-hand combat. One type of club had a circular head: fashioned from stone or metal, it had six projecting points. Battle-axes with stone or bronze heads were also used. Some non-Inca soldiers preferred their own traditional weapons. The Colla, for example, tied three stones to a cord: when the cord was thrown, it entangled the legs of the enemy. Coastal tribes favored spear throwers and dart throwers.

The Four Quarters

Tahuantinsuyu was the name given by the Incas to their empire. The boundary lines, which ran roughly northwest to southeast and northeast to southwest, originated in the main square of the sacred city of Cuzco. Collasuyu, which lay in the south, was the largest quarter. The second-largest quarter was Chinchaysuyu. Antisuyu and Cuntisuyu were relatively small. Each quarter was subdivided into smaller provinces.

Administration

A meticulously organized system ensured the smooth running of Tahuantinsuyu. At the height of the empire, more than ten million people lived within its borders. Of these, fewer than 40,000 were of Inca descent. New territories were ruled from newly built towns with Inca-trained officials. After each military victory, access roads were built; engineers and census takers surveyed and calculated the land-holdings and resources of subject populations so that taxes could be imposed. Although the Incas rarely disturbed the basic pattern of life, inhabitants were required to comply with Inca laws and with sun worship. As the Incas spread their rule, the languages spoken within their empire increased. An official tongue was therefore imposed: after 1438, Quechua became the language of administration. By these various means, the Incas governed more than 80 political provinces.

Although unified into a single state, Tahuantinsuyu was divided into four areas (marked by dotted lines). At the center lay the city of Cuzco. A complex network of roads (in blue) linked all parts of the empire. The longest was the Andean Road, which ran through the mountains.

The Empire Observed

Inca civilization was at its in height when Spanish forces reached Peru in 1532. Much of what we know about the Inca empire is based on the written reports of Spanish observers. Fortunately, the Incas have left us their own version of events. All these accounts help us to tell the Inca story. Included in this book are several sixteenth-century illustrations by Felipe Guamán Poma de Ayala, a native Andean. They show scenes from Inca history, religion, and daily life and serve as a very valuable source of information.

The empire relied on a carefully planned communications system. More than 15,500 mi. (25,000 km) of roads linked different provinces and passed through all types of landscape. Ravines and rivers were crossed by suspension bridges. Distances were marked out at regular intervals, and travelers could rest in roadside shelters. Armies moved along well-kept, all-weather highways to calm disturbances and crush rebellions. Important messages were carried by relays of high-speed runners. Trained from boyhood, they kept Cuzco informed of events throughout Tahuantinsuyu. Runners were stationed in pairs in stone huts: while one man slept the other waited, ready to run to the next post about 1.5 mi. (2.43 km) away.

The remains of the old Inca roads can still be seen today. This road passes through Chachapoyas in modern-day Peru. The Incas used roads to transport food and other commodities.

CHAPTER 4

Politics and Society

The Ruling Class

Inca social organization was very structured and can be visualized as a pyramid. The role of each person was clearly defined. At the top of the pyramid was the Inca royal family: members of a hereditary aristocracy, they could trace their family back to Manco Capac, founder of the Inca dynasty. The royal family enjoyed many privileges. Allowed to wear special clothing, members lived in splendor in Cuzco. They alone could serve as high priests, and they alone could command the army. The head of state was the emperor. He was supported by a supreme council of four prefects called Apus. Chosen from the highest nobility, each was responsible for one of the four quarters of the kingdom.

The Sapa Inca

The emperor's official title was Sapa Inca, or Unique Inca. Worshiped as the "Divine Son of the Sun," his power was absolute: as the Sun ruled the skies, so the Sapa Inca ruled on Earth. Everything—the people, the land, and all its riches—belonged to him. The wife of the Sapa Inca was known as the Coya. By long tradition, she was also his full sister.

▼ This drinking cup of painted wood shows an Inca nobleman. Because of their massive gold ear plugs, Inca nobles were nicknamed Orejones, meaning "big ears," by the Spaniards. Goblets of this type were used during important religious rituals.

In addition to the Coya, the emperor kept many other wives and concubines. Rules for the choice of heirs were strict: only sons born to the Coya could inherit the Incaship. Each Inca ruler built his own palace in the center of Cuzco. These were low stone structures: roofed with thatch, they enclosed a number of courtyards. The emperor's own quarters were situated in the heart of the palace: walls were adorned with gold and silver and were hung with magnificent textiles. At the death of each Inca, his palace was sealed off to become his tomb.

The Empress

The Coya had her own palace in Cuzco, where she lived with her ladies in waiting. She was respected, and she actively supported religion and took part in prayers and ceremonies. The Cult of the Moon was dedicated to her. The Coya's garden contained a wide range of plants and animals. When she left the palace, the Coya walked beneath a feathered canopy hung with silver ornaments; servants covered the ground in front of her with fine cloths.

▲ This picture of Huayna Capac shows the emperor wearing a patterned tunic without sleeves, a cloak, and a military helmet.

Life for the elite in Cuzco was governed by complicated ritual. This account, written by the Spaniard Pedro Cieza de León, described the life of the emperor: "From many of the lords of the country there came emissaries every day bringing gifts; the court was filled with nobles, and his palaces with vessels of gold and silver and other great treasures. In the morning he took his meal, and from noon until late in the day he gave audience, accompanied by his guard, to whoever wished to talk with him. He spent the rest of the day, until it was night, drinking; then he dined by the light of wood...." We know from sources such as this one that the nobility ate tropical fruits, fresh meat, fish, and wild duck. These delicacies were brought to Cuzco from different regions by runners.

Antisuyu

Acllahuasi

Sacsahuaman

Tullamayo River (canalized)

Huatanay River
(canalized)

Coricancha

Huacapata

Cuntisuyu

▲ As this map shows, Cuzco was planned to resemble the shape of a giant puma. The great shrine-fortress of Sacsahuaman was the puma's head. The tail lay at the point where the two canalized rivers met. The Sun Temple, or Coricancha, was in the puma's tail.

Cuzco

The imperial capital was believed by the Incas to be the "Navel of the World." Although Cuzco began as a small township, it was reorganized and enlarged during the reign of Pachacuti. This carefully planned city was the heart of Tahuantinsuyu. Starting out from the main square, boundary lines quartered the empire and the city. Around this central plaza, called Huacapata (Holy Place), were the palaces of the Sapa Inca and his predecessors. Other important buildings off the Huacapata included the Yachahuasi, where the sons of the nobility were educated, and the Acllahuasi (House of the Chosen Women and Guardian Mothers). The Sun Temple was the most important religious building in the empire. Sheets of gold covered its gateways, and it had a series of chambers arranged around a courtyard.

▶ Cuzco is situated approximately 11,680 ft. (3,560 m) above sea level. Set in a highland basin, it is ringed with mountain peaks. Although this illustration was made after the arrival of the Spaniards, it gives an idea of the orderly appearance of the old Inca capital. In Inca times, by some estimates, the inner city contained about 4,000 buildings. It covered an area about 6,570 ft. by 1,640 ft. (2,000 m by 500 m).

CVS. CO.

CVSCO REGNI PERV IN NOVO ORBE CAPVT

The chief entrances to Cuzco were marked by great gateways, where guards monitored the comings and goings of all subjects. Entry into Cuzco was forbidden between sunset and sunrise. The inner city was inhabited only by the Sapa Inca and by members of the nobility: these included priests and important government officials.

The long and narrow streets of Cuzco were paved; water was carried along their centers by stone-lined drainage channels. The capital was dominated by the fortress-shrine of Sacsahuaman: if trouble threatened, Cuzco's inhabitants could take refuge behind its massive walls. The Incas excelled as builders. Using large blocks of stone, shaped so that they fitted perfectly together, they designed their chief buildings to resist the earthquakes that constantly threatened Cuzco. Less important constructions were made of stone set in mud mortar, or of adobe (unfired mud bricks). Most Inca structures had a single story, and roofs were thatched.

▲ The shrine-fortress of Sacsahuaman was perched high on a hill overlooking the main part of Cuzco. The military occupied two towers; the third was furnished as a royal residence. Sacsahuaman also served as a temple of sacrifice and prayer.

Cuzco lies in the triangle formed by two rivers: the Huatanay and the Tullamayo. These were straightened and turned into canals by the Incas to form an acute angle. Four main roads led from the city to the provinces. The basic layout of Cuzco was adapted for use in major towns across the Inca empire. Built by the public workforce, the towns each had a central plaza designed for enormous gatherings. Only Cuzco took the form of a giant puma, however. It seems likely that the Incas learned the art of town planning from the Chimú or from the builders of Tiahuanaco.

▼ A herd of llamas near Sucre in modern Peru. Today, as in the past, llamas are crucial to the Andean way of life: they are raised for their wool and used as pack animals.

Ordinary People

The power of the elite was passed down from generation to generation. But ordinary people had few rights, and one all-important duty: to work for the state. In return, the state guaranteed them the necessities of life. Throughout the empire, each individual, from the top of the social hierarchy to the bottom, had a clearly defined role. Every aspect of life was controlled. Law-abiding subjects were looked after until the end of their lives, but those who failed in their duties were punished. Outside the capital, most commoners lived in farming and herding communities. The Inca state relied on its rural populations to grow food and to raise llamas. Land, herds, and produce were divided into three equal parts. One third was set aside for the cult of the Sun, while another third went to the emperor: religion and government were thus supported by taxation. The third and last share went to the peasants.

Governors and Officials

Tahuantinsuyu, with its many divisions and sub-divisions, required many administrators. As already mentioned, the Sapa Inca was the supreme head of the empire. Beneath him, four Apus (prefects) represented Tahuantinsuyu's four quarters, but resided in Cuzco. The various provinces were ruled in the emperor's name by the Tocricoc Apus. These were imperial governors who lived in great luxury in the provincial capitals. All these posts were filled by members of the royal ayllus, who were Incas by blood.

Below this administrative level, positions were often filled by non-Incas. The Curacas were the native rulers or chiefs of conquered territories. Regarded as a secondary nobility, they were allowed to keep their authority over local populations. In return, they obeyed Inca laws and followed their customs. Curacas were required to spend fixed periods of time in Cuzco and to send their sons to be educated there. Posts were hereditary, but the status of each Curaca was determined by the number of tax-paying householders in his charge. To help them carry out their responsibilities, Curacas appointed local foremen known as Camayocs, who worked as district leaders. A close check was kept on the workings of the state by other civil servants. Inspectors, whose Quechua name meant "he whom nothing escapes," toured the empire. They monitored the lives of private citizens and reported back to the capital on matters of taxation and administration.

TRAVAXA 3ARAPAPAHALLMAIMITA

▲ The rural population of Tahuantinsuyu was divided into many small farming and pastoral communities. This illustration shows peasants tending their fields. The Inca economy rested on the shoulders of common taxpayers, because it was their labor that produced the food and goods needed to sustain the empire.

The social structure of Tahuantinsuyu depended on the ayllu as the basic unit of organization. Borrowed by the Incas from the Aymara people, the word "ayllu" described a family clan living self-sufficiently (from their own produce). At birth, each ayllu member inherited a set of relationships and responsibilities. Royal ayllus were formed by the descendants of each emperor.

▼ Deriving its name from the word "knot," the quipu enabled the Incas to record information. Long quipus reached over 10 ft. (3 m) and had more than 2,000 strings.

Taxation

Throughout Tahuantinsuyu, taxes were calculated in terms of work. Each province was required to contribute fixed amounts of food and goods to the state. Within each province, and within each ayllu, householders were organized to meet these commitments. In the absence of writing, quipus (knotted cords) were used for record keeping. When a new region was conquered, its resources were calculated: a list was made of lands and herds, and the labor force was counted.

Inca laws required everyone, whether young or old, to carry out tasks appropriate to their sex, age, and strength. Agricultural duties were performed by male and female subjects. In addition, men were often sent to serve the state in distant territories, and women were responsible for weaving cloth at home. Light work was done by the disabled, by children, and by the elderly. Their tasks included gathering brushwood and corn husking. The duty of all commoners was to work for the good of government and religion. Tribute payments of food, cloth, tools, and other vital supplies were kept in storehouses. These were built in regular rows on the hillsides near major towns.

Administrators organized the empire by using the quipu. This clever device consisted of a length of cord held horizontally. From it, strings of various colors were suspended vertically. The Incas used a decimal system for counting. Numbers, laws, historic events, and other information were indicated by knots of different sizes, colors, and positions on the strings. Quipus were tied and "read" by specially appointed officials. Known as Quipucamayocs (Quipu Keepers), they kept a list of the population, produce, herds, and weapons throughout the empire.

The Sapa Inca represented the Sun on Earth. Within his empire, all men were regarded as his sons, and all women as his wives. In return for total obedience, the Sapa Inca gave his subjects lifelong security. The material needs of each family were taken care of. In times of famine and hardship, grain was taken from the emperor's storehouses and given to the hungry. The old and the disabled were fed and clothed; their welfare was the subject of a "Poor Law," which provided the needy with the necessities of life. Subjects traveling on official business were supplied with free food and lodging in roadside shelters.

Mit'a Service

Because Inca subjects paid taxes with their labor, they were classified according to age and physical condition. Laws governed the fair distribution of work. Group labor projects, often far from home, were called "mit'a." For fixed periods, able-bodied male taxpayers provided the human resources needed for road building, canal digging, mining, and construction work. They also had to serve as soldiers.

▲ The Incas overcame the steepness of Andean mountain slopes by building terraces for the intensive growing of crops. For this important work, a large and highly organized labor force was needed. Often terraces were made by male subjects on mit'a service to the state. As this photograph shows, terracing is still used by some Andean farmers in Peru. It is also found in other parts of the world where steep hillsides make normal agriculture impossible.

CHAPTER 5

Ideas and Religion

The Power of the Emperor

For the Incas, government and religion were closely linked. Sun worship was central to Inca culture, along with deep respect for the dead. Because Manco Capac and his descendants were officially the sons of Inti, they ruled by divine right. Each was worshiped as a god during his lifetime. When an emperor died, it was said that the Sun had recalled him. He was accompanied on his journey to the other world by servants and female companions. It is unclear, however, whether they gave up their lives willingly or were murdered. A long period of mourning followed the death of each Sapa Inca. His body, preserved to ensure his continuing presence on Earth, was maintained in splendor in his own palace. Even in death, he was consulted as an oracle by his people.

Spanish observers described the lifelike appearance of dead rulers. Garcilaso de la Vega, the son of a Spaniard and an Inca princess, wrote down his memories of imperial Cuzco. As a youth, he had seen the mummies of three sovereigns: kept in a sitting position, they were "perfect as life, without so much as a hair of an eyebrow missing." When he touched the finger of Huayna Capac, it "seemed like that of a wooden statue, it was so hard and stiff."

▼ As shown here, the mummified remains of dead emperors were brought into the open on important feast days. The remains were clothed in their best finery and paraded before the public on decorated litters.

After the death of the Sapa Inca, his entrails were removed and buried, but his body was preserved through various drying procedures. The eyes were replaced with replicas made of inlaid shells. More than 1,000 years earlier, the people of Paracas had also mummified their dead. Dressed in fine fabrics and surrounded by precious objects, each dead emperor remained in his own palace where he was waited on and worshiped.

The Acllas

Selected for their beauty, Acllas (Chosen Women) could be of royal blood or peasant stock. In each province, a high-ranking official called the Apupanaca was responsible for inspecting all girls who had reached the age of ten. Those with great qualities were sent to convents called Acllahuasi. There they were taught by Mamacunas (Guardian Mothers). Lessons centered on religion and arts such as spinning, weaving, and cooking.

When they were 13 or 14, girls were taken by the Apupanaca to Cuzco. They were seen by the emperor, who decided on the future of each. Some were destined for sacrifice. Others were selected to lead lives of purity—serving in temples and shrines, or teaching future generations of Acllas in the Acllahuasi. The loveliest girls became secondary wives or servants to the emperor himself, or were given by the emperor as a mark of favor to Inca nobles, Curacas, and successful warriors.

▲ This photograph shows a human head of carved wood. Wrapped in woven cloth, it has eyes of shell inlay. Once this head was part of an Inca mummy bundle. It has been dated by archaeologists between A.D. 1100 and A.D. 1400.

Sun Worship

Inti, the Sun god, was worshiped as the "Giver of Life."
By helping the crops to mature, the Sun allowed
humans to survive. The Incas saw themselves as Inti's
chosen people, or "Children of the Sun." Their emperor,
the Sapa Inca, was Inti's representative on Earth: his
other title was Intip Churin (Son of the Sun). In this role
he had charge of the temples and estates of the Sun.

During the reign of Pachacuti, the cult of the Sun
grew stronger. According to Inca
legend, Inti appeared before the
young Pachacuti in a vision.
Inspired and guided by the Sun,
Pachacuti went on to extend and
replan the Inca empire. When he
rebuilt Cuzco, he ordered
construction of the Coricancha
(House of the Sun). Throughout
Tahuantinsuyu, newly conquered
populations were given
instruction in Sun worship, and
Sun temples were erected in
provincial centers.

Viracocha

Viracocha was regarded by the
Incas as the creator of the world.
They believed that this supreme
deity had caused the sun to rise
from the waters of Lake Titicaca.
Tiahuanaco was inhabited at this time by a
race of giants. Viracocha turned the giants to
stone. Then, he collected clay from the lake and modeled
animals and people. He painted the human figures with
different kinds of clothing and taught them different
languages and customs. When he had finished, Viracocha
told these new human beings to go underground and
to emerge separately from lakes, hills, springs, and caves.

▲ This figure of stone
was carved between
A.D. 600 and A.D. 1200 at
Tiahuanaco, in present-
day Bolivia. It is thought
to show the god
Viracocha.

◄ At Pachacamac, on the Peruvian coast, the Incas established an important temple of the Sun. Set on the sacred site of a pre-Inca cult, it was associated with Viracocha. Adjoining the temple was the Acllahuasi, or House of the Chosen Women and Guardian Mothers. Builders used local materials: adobe and stucco were covered with painted decoration.

They did this, settling in different homelands. The Incas, as we have seen, were led out of a Peruvian cave by Manco Capac. Through their belief in Viracocha, the Incas explained the creation of human beings and described how so many different groups of people arrived in the Andes.

In Cuzco, Viracocha was represented by images or symbols in the great Coricancha, yet he seems to have been a mysterious god. Inca accounts suggest that he was invisible and unknowable. Viracocha was connected with the earth, water, and the coast.

The following lines, written in the sixteenth century by Pedro de Sarmiento de Gamboa, explain how the Sun was fed by the Mamacunas (Guardian Mothers). They offered "much richly cooked food to the image or idol of the Sun; then they put the food into a great fire on an altar." Liquor was offered in the same way. "The chief of the Mamacunas saluted the Sun with a small vase, and the rest was thrown on the fire. In addition, many jars full of that liquor were poured into a trough which had a drain, all being offerings to the Sun."

▼ This Inca figurine of gold is thought to show a Mamacuna (Guardian Mother). Mamacunas taught the Acllas (Chosen Women) and served in temples and shrines. Some became the concubines of the Inca emperor. The figurine is wrapped in a woven textile fastened with a gold pin. Sacred objects of this type were often placed in Inca burials.

The Coricancha

Images of Inti were kept in the Coricancha (House of the Sun) in Cuzco. When Spanish forces arrived in Peru in the sixteenth century, they saw the Coricancha at the height of its splendor. Pedro Cieza de León wrote: "The stone appeared to me to be of a dusky or black color…. The wall had many openings, and the doorways were well carved. Around the wall, halfway up, there was a band of gold…. The doorways and doors were covered with plates of the same metal. Within were four houses, not very large, but with walls of the same kind and covered with plates of gold within and without… In one of these houses, which was the richest, there was the figure of the Sun, very large and made of gold, very ingeniously worked, and enriched with many precious stones…."

Other Deities

Other important Inca gods included Pacha Mama (Mother Earth), Cuichi (the Rainbow), and Mama Cocha (Mother Water). Illapa was Lord of Thunder, Lightning, Rain, and Hail. He was regarded as the messenger of the Sun. Prayers for rain were addressed to him, and shrines for his worship were built in many places. In Cuzco, Illapa's image was placed beside that of Inti in the Coricancha. Mama Quilla (the Moon) was worshiped as the sister-wife of the Sun. Shrines to the Moon were ornamented with silver and served by priestesses. In the Coricancha, her image was housed in a special silver-clad chamber.

Priests and Priestesses

The priesthood was organized according to a strict hierarchy. At its head was the Uillac Uma (Highest Priest). Like his main assistants, he belonged to the royal family.

Below the Highest Priest were ten Hatun Uillca: each was responsible for one of the ten religious regions of Tahuantinsuyu. Next came the ordinary priests, known as the Yana Uillca. Important shrines were looked after by priests of various ranks, but small shrines had just one attendant. Some sources suggest that priests were allowed to marry.

Women also had their place in the religious hierarchy. After their education in the Acllahuasi, large numbers of Acllas were chosen by the emperor for religious service. Some became priestesses of the Moon, while others were dedicated to the Sun. Sun Virgins lived as recluses and carried out various sacred tasks. There were approximately 1,500 Sun Virgins in Cuzco, under the leadership of a high priestess. Their duties included weaving cloth and food preparation for the Sun.

▼ For the Incas and their predecessors, the natural world was alive with supernatural forces. This Moche jar shows three corn cobs with faces.

The Inca system of taxation obliged men and women to give their labor. One third of that labor upheld the religious structure of Tahuantinsuyu. By cultivating the lands and tending the herds of the Sun, peasants supported the Acllahuasi, the priesthood, and the shrine attendants. Food and other supplies were kept in the storehouses of the Sun. Much of this produce was required for religious sacrifices, ceremonies, and public festivals.

The Afterlife

The Incas believed in an afterlife. Virtuous individuals joined the Sun in Hanacpacha (the Upper World), but sinners were destined to suffer cold and hunger in the depths of the earth. Even after death, contact was maintained with the living. It was the duty of descendants to honor and look after the remains of dead ancestors. If these sacred obligations were fulfilled, then the dead were thought to have a good influence over the health and well-being of the living. Stones set in clay were often used to build tombs: these were positioned in crevices along cliff faces or in rock shelters. The dead were wrapped in their best clothes and mats and placed in a sitting position. For their journey to the afterlife, they were given food and selected objects. In the case of a warrior, these included his weapons. After burial, the entrance to the tomb was blocked. Sometimes several members of the same family were buried together.

Huacas

The Incas worshiped sacred sites known as huacas. Because the landscape was thought to be alive with supernatural forces, huacas were often caves, quarries, boulders, and springs. Some sacred places had historical or mythological associations. Manco Capac, according to legend, turned to stone after founding Cuzco and establishing a family. This ancestral stone was worshiped by all Incas. Other huacas included major battle sites, temples, stone boundary markers, and the burial places of important people.

▲ Felipe Guamán Poma de Ayala illustrated the different burial practices of Tahuantinsuyu. Shown here is a large tomb built above ground.

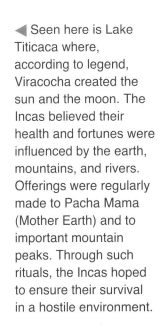
◀ Seen here is Lake Titicaca where, according to legend, Viracocha created the sun and the moon. The Incas believed their health and fortunes were influenced by the earth, mountains, and rivers. Offerings were regularly made to Pacha Mama (Mother Earth) and to important mountain peaks. Through such rituals, the Incas hoped to ensure their survival in a hostile environment.

The Incas had a system of imaginary lines or rays called ceques. Ceques radiated from Cuzco's Coricancha temple and stretched to the farthest horizons. Huacas lay on these imaginary lines. The term *huaca* was also applied to portable objects such as amulets and figurines in the shape of people, plants, and animals. Thought to offer protection, they were regarded as sacred. Huacas from conquered provinces were often kept in the Coricancha in Cuzco. After a military victory, the Incas were anxious to integrate new subjects into the religious system of Tahuantinsuyu: subdued populations were therefore required by law to send one of their most hallowed objects to the "Navel of the World."

Spanish observers did not fully understand how the Incas saw the universe. For the Incas, the cosmos represented a balance among different forces. It was this idea that led them to divide their empire into four parts. Cuzco, "Navel of the World," was divided into two: Hanan Cuzco (Upper Cuzco) was the front part of the puma, and Hurin Cuzco (Lower Cuzco) was the hind part.

Space and Time

Modern researchers sometimes compare the Coricancha to the center of a universal dial. Forty-one ceques, the imaginary lines described on page 33, radiated out from the Coricancha, like the spokes of a wheel. They passed approximately 328 huacas (sacred sites), and this allowed the Incas to track the movements of the sun, the moon, and the stars. Stone towers were erected on high locations along ceques. By watching the sun appear on these towers, the Incas calculated the seasons of the agricultural year.

▼ This golden mask shows the face of Inti, the Sun God. Worshiped as the "Giver of Life," Inti made the crops grow. Farmers organized their activities in accordance with the solar calendar of 12 months. One third of all fertile land and herds in Tahuantisuyu belonged to the Sun.

The Cosmos and the Calendar

Inca astronomers used a solar calendar of 12 months; all their farming and agricultural decisions were based on this. They also counted 12 lunar months: these phases showed the Incas the best time for planting.

EL TER3ERO MES MAR3O
PACH IADVM

◀ A priest prepares to sacrifice a llama. Many llamas from the Sun's herds were killed during religious festivals and ceremonies.

Venus was the chief representative of the stars. Stars, regarded as the children of the Sun and Moon, influenced the development of crops and herds. Of great importance was the Milky Way: the largest of the heavenly bodies, it was called Mayu (Celestial River). Inca astronomers thought that Mayu traveled each year along two crossing axes that divided the heavens into four quarters. The landscape of Tahuantinsuyu, the Land of the Four Quarters, reflected this arrangement: the boundary lines echoed the heavenly axes.

Sacrifice

The Incas viewed all misfortune as having been caused by sins against nature or the social order. The goodwill of their deities was won with sacrifices. Although human lives were sometimes offered to the gods, more common by far were sacrifices involving llamas and guinea pigs. Animals had to be free of blemishes. Brown animals were offered to Viracocha, white ones to the Sun, mottled ones to Thunder. Sacrifices were made every day to the Sun as it rose over Cuzco.

Human sacrifices were made at times of national emergency or during the coronation of the emperor. The victims included girls from the Acllahuasi, and ten-year-old boys taken as taxation from the fathers of large families. Occasionally, during major festivals, small infants were also sacrificed: by giving up their life force it was thought that the life force of the ruler would be strengthened.

The Incas watched the sun, moon, and stars for signs about their future. Eclipses and falling stars were regarded as bad omens; so were earthquakes and tidal waves. Omens were interpreted, and dreams were analyzed by diviners. The sacrifice of animals played a key role in the Inca world: by studying the entrails, the Incas thought they could foretell the outcome of battles and other events. Some individuals went on long pilgrimages to consult special oracles, while others visited nearby huacas.

Feasts of the Sun

In the Southern Hemisphere, the winter solstice falls in June. Each year, the Incas celebrated the return of the sun during Inti Raymi (Feast of the Sun). After a three-day fast, they gathered to greet the dawn. In Cuzco, the emperor and members of his family presided over sacrifices: children were buried alive with llamas and with vessels of gold and silver. Inti's rays, caught in a golden bowl, were directed onto a bundle of cotton threads: a flame was kindled and guarded until the following year by the Sun Virgins of the Coricancha.

Capac Raymi (Magnificent Festival) was held in December during the summer solstice. Poised above the Intihuatana (sun stone) at midday, the sun cast no shadows. As during Inti Raymi, celebrations included the sacrifice of gold, silver, and infants. In December, the provinces of Tahuantinsuyu sent their produce to Cuzco for the emperor and for religion. This was also the time when puberty rites, called Huarachico, were held for the sons of noblemen and commoners.

Other Festivals

Capac Raymi marked the start of the Inca year; there followed a month dedicated to the Moon. Puberty rites, with dances and sacrifices, continued during this period. February was the month of the "Great Ripening": gifts of gold and silver were offered to the Sun, the Moon, and other deities. In March, the month of the autumn equinox, the Incas celebrated "Earth Ripening." The Festival of the Sapa Inca took place in April, under the auspices of the Sun. During one April ceremony, members of the royal dynasty sang to a white llama: dressed in royal clothing, it represented the first llama on Earth.

▼ At the highest point of the famous Inca city of Machu Picchu stands the carved Intihuatana stone. Its name means "Tethering Post of the Sun." Probably used for astronomical rituals, it celebrated the sun and connected the earth with the heavens.

Because the empire depended on farming, agricultural activities were treated with respect. Rituals and ceremonies initiated each phase of the agricultural year. These were often presided over by the emperor himself. In July, when it was time to plow the earth, the Sapa Inca used a golden taclla (hand plow) to make a symbolic furrow. Nobles, priests, and high officials all took their turn digging.

▲ As in Inca times, corn is still a staple crop. This Peruvian farmer in the Chancay Valley relies on a good corn harvest to support her family.

In May, the month of the "Great Cultivation," the Incas celebrated the corn harvest: many llamas were sacrificed, and great feasts were held.

Inti Raymi, described earlier, dominated the month of June. July was known as the "Plowing Month." During August, the "Sowing Month," sacrifices were made to the huacas. Mama Huaco, the mother of Manco Capac, was regarded as the patroness of agriculture, so corn was ritually sown in all fields assigned to her. Sacrifices were then made to Water, Air, Frost, and the Sun. The "Feast of the Moon," which took place in September during the spring equinox, was very popular with women. It too provided an occasion for feasting and dancing. During the month of October, peasants watched over their crops and held ceremonies to increase rainfall. In November, during the "Festival of the Dead," the dead were brought out in public and offered food and gifts. With Capac Raymi, the new cycle began once again.

CHAPTER 6

Art, Science, and Entertainment

The House of Teaching

Education was compulsory for the privileged classes. Studies began at 15 and lasted for four years. Lessons were given by Amautas (Wise Men) in the Yachahuasi (House of Teaching) in Cuzco. Pupils studied the Quechua language, religion, record keeping with quipus, and history. Other subjects included poetry, music, geometry, geography, and astronomy. The sons of commoners received no formal education: they copied their parents' skills. No girls received educations, unless they were to enter the Acllahuasi.

Language and Song

The Incas allowed conquered peoples to keep their own languages, but Quechua was the official language of Tahuantinsuyu. Poems, legends, and prayers were passed on orally. It was the duty of the Amautas to collect and preserve Inca history and tradition. Stories were set to verse by bards.

▼ Because musical instruments were often made from materials that rotted, almost none have survived from the Cuzco region. This bone flute is from the north coast of Peru. Probably Moche, it has a bird-shaped head.

After the arrival of the Spaniards and the introduction of writing, some verses were recorded. These lines, recorded by Pedro de Sarmiento de Gamboa, were part of a poem on the death of Pachacuti:

"I was born like a lily in the garden,
And so also was I brought up.
As my age came, I have grown up,
And, as I had to die, so I dried up,
And I died. "

Music

The Incas had no stringed instruments, only wind and percussion. Wind instruments included flutes and clay whistles. The quena flute, which consisted of a single joint of cane, had up to eight finger stops; panpipes were made by tying together different lengths of cane. Inca melodies were based on the five-note scale. In war, bone flutes and conch-shell trumpets were used. Drums came in various sizes: some, sounded during victory marches, were made from the skins of enemy warriors. Important ceremonies and displays of public worship included dances. Performers wore elaborate costumes. They used anklets of seeds or snail shells, and small bells of silver, copper, or bronze.

▲ This silver figure is playing the panpipes. Today Andean musicians still play the panpipes.

Organized games were a part of ceremonial life. During puberty ceremonies, 14-year-old boys of high rank took part in athletic contests: they ran races, fought mock battles, and underwent endurance tests. As adults, members of the Inca elite often went on hunting expeditions. They also gambled with dice. During one game of chance, Topa Inca (the tenth emperor) accepted a challenge from his son: when he lost, he gave his son the governorship of the province of his choice.

Professional Artisans

Luxury goods were created by specialists who worked full time for the emperor or for other members of the elite. Their job was usually hereditary, and they lived in cities. Included in this category were metalsmiths, potters, carpenters, jewelry makers, featherworkers, and experts in weaving and embroidery. In return for their highly skilled work, artists and their families were supported; they were provided with tools and with the best raw materials.

Textiles

Weaving was a well-respected art in Inca times. Women in each household spun and wove: they provided their families with clothing, and the emperor with tribute. Cloth was stored in vast quantities in the warehouses of Tahuantinsuyu. It was needed by the state for distribution to the armies and the labor force. Gifts of clothing were made by the emperor to friends and to people whom he wished to reward.

Luxury cloth was produced by specialist male weavers, and by the Mamacunas (Guardian Mothers). They worked with wool taken from llama or alpaca herds and from wild vicuña or guanaco. Cotton was also used.

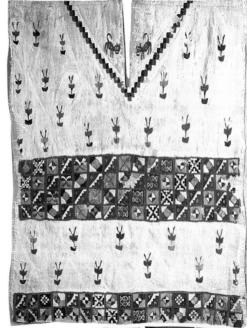

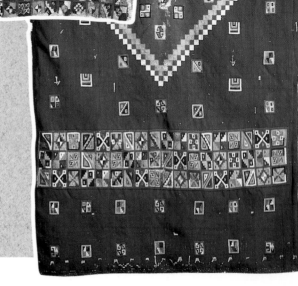

◀▼ These magnificent men's tunics were woven more than 500 years ago on the south coast of Peru. Geometric designs, of the style seen here, were worn only by people of high status. One tunic is also decorated with plants and feline animals.

◀ This featherwork tunic was made more than 1,000 years ago by the Nazca or Huari peoples. It is richly patterned with designs showing the Sun god and a dragonlike creature with two heads. The makers used red, blue, and yellow macaw feathers and flamingo feathers of deep pink.

Although every known weaving technique was used in ancient Peru, tapestry methods were often employed for important Inca textiles. Inca designs were often intricate and included geometric patterns. Royal and religious textiles, in a vast range of natural dyes, were sometimes decorated with gold and silver ornaments and featherwork.

Clothing

Clothing indicated the wearer's social status and place of origin. Women wore a long, sleeveless dress secured by a waist sash and a shoulder mantle fastened by a pin. Male clothing consisted of a loincloth, a sleeveless tunic, and a cloak. Although these garments were simply made, those of the elite displayed rich colors and complex patterns. Vicuña wool was often used by the emperor. He wore the llauta, insignia of his supreme power. This was a braid of many colors, wound several times around the head. From it hung a royal fringe of red tassels and gold tubes.

Weaving is the interlacing of two sets of threads at right angles. In Tahuantinsuyu, most weavers produced cloth on the back-strap loom. Still in use today, the back-strap loom requires that the threads be stretched horizontally between two bars: while one bar is tied to a tree or post, the other is attached by a strap to the weaver. With this method, the width of cloth is limited by the weaver's armspan. Occasionally, vertical looms were used to produce wider textiles.

Sweat of the Sun, Tears of the Moon

The Incas regarded gold as being related to the sun, and silver to the moon. Gold was also the symbolic color of the emperor; silver represented the Coya. These precious metals, poetically described in Quechua as the "Sweat of the Sun" and the "Tears of the Moon," were the sacred property of the emperor. Silver was plentiful in Peru, and gold was extracted from the steep hills east of Lake Titicaca. Strict laws governed operations: mining was carried out by able-bodied taxpayers on mit'a service; production was recorded by officials using quipus. Gold and silver went directly to Cuzco, and it is said that 7 million ounces (almost 200 tons) of gold may have entered the capital each year.

 The Incas regarded gold and silver as sacred. The gold human figure and silver beaker shown here were found by archaeologists in Peru. They show the skills possessed by ancient metalsmiths in the region.

The following lines, written by Garcilaso de la Vega, described the garden of the Sapa Inca:
"There were fields of corn with silver stalks and golden ears, on which the leaves, grains, and even the corn silk were shown. In addition, there were all kinds of gold and silver animals in these gardens, such as rabbits, mice, lizards, snakes, butterflies, foxes, and wildcats; there were birds set in the trees, and others bent over the flowers, breathing in their nectar."

Gold and silver were reserved for luxury and ceremonial objects. Like the Chimú, the Incas were highly skilled metalsmiths. They knew how to hammer metal into thin sheets, creating a raised pattern on the reverse side. Inca metalsmiths also knew how to solder, and how to cast in molds. Gold was melted in a furnace. According to Garcilaso de la Vega, goldsmiths "went around the fire, blowing it with tubes."

Although commoners were rarely allowed to wear elaborate jewelry, fine objects were worn by the elite. Male symbols of status included wide bracelets as well as metal breast ornaments, awarded for bravery to warriors. Because of their massive ear plugs of gold, Inca nobles were nicknamed *Orejones*, meaning "big ears," by the Spaniards. In Cuzco, gold embellished musical instruments, weapons, and royal litters. The Coricancha, or House of the Sun, was known as the "Golden Place": it sparkled on all sides with gold. In the gardens belonging to the Sun and the emperor, plants and animals were reproduced in gold and silver.

Copper, tin, and platinum were also mined by the Incas. Metalsmiths cast copper and bronze (a mixture of copper and tin) to obtain tools and weapons. "White gold" was an alloy of platinum, gold, and silver.

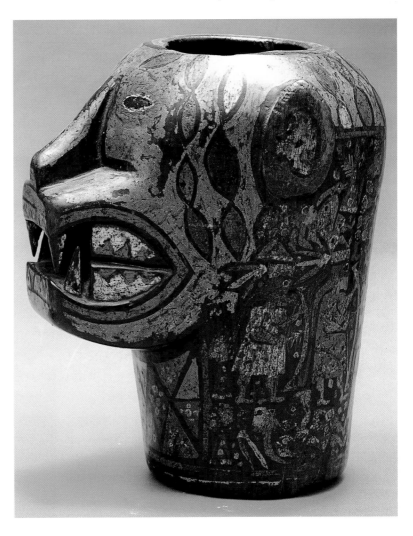

▲ This drinking vessel was used by the Incas during religious ceremonies and rituals. It is shaped like the head of a jaguar or puma and is painted with designs.

Inca Architecture

The Incas excelled as engineers and stonemasons. Spurred on by their vision of imperial grandeur, they used their vast labor force to create imposing cities that could withstand the threat of earthquakes and survive the passage of time. Buildings and public works were planned by architects and engineers of royal status.

Inca architecture was characterized by its simplicity and solidity. Using a minimum of tools, the Incas erected massive buildings with little ornamentation or sculpture. Walls were composed of vast granite blocks. These fitted together so closely that no mortar was needed: even today, a knife could not be inserted between them. Occasionally, buildings had a second story. Timber-framed roofs thatched with Ichu grass sloped to allow the highland rain to run off them. Although the floors of important structures were paved or laid with small pebbles, most buildings had floors of beaten earth.

The Crest of the Andes

Machu Picchu, situated high on a narrow ridge of rock, is the best preserved of all the Inca cities. Because it was protected on three sides by steep slopes and a mountain, it was a natural fortress. Today, as in the past, visitors enter from the south along the Inca road.

Machu Picchu was organized in the same manner as other provincial cities. Flanking the central plaza were the Sun Temple, the Acllahuasi, and various public buildings. A gateway linked the Sun Temple to the royal palace. Baths and fountains were supplied by an efficient water system.

▼ Main picture Machu Picchu, in the High Andes of Peru, is the best preserved of all Inca cities.

▼ Inset Inca walls were made of large granite blocks. Shown here is an example of stonework from the shrine fortress of Sacsahuaman.

The city included a defensive wall, temples, an observatory, dwellings, storehouses, and burial caves modified with masonry. Hillsides were terraced for the intensive cultivation of crops.

Aerial photographs show how Inca engineers made use of natural features when planning Machu Picchu. Because the Incas worshiped the earth and regarded the landscape as sacred, their architecture was designed to harmonize with the mountainous scenery of their homeland.

In the damp atmosphere of the Andes, stone was the most hardwearing building material. Thousands of laborers split and transported giant blocks of rock with the help of cables and wooden rollers. These blocks were shaped with stone hammers. If a smooth surface was required, blocks were polished with sand and water. At Sacsahuaman, some building blocks were over 26 ft. (8 m) high, and weighed more than 200 tons. Inca stonemasons could build a wall without mortar or cement. These highly valued craftsmen were sent to different construction sites to instruct the local labor force.

CHAPTER 7

The Pattern of Rural Life

Farming in a Hostile Environment

Outside the towns and cities of Tahuantinsuyu, most Inca subjects lived in farming and pastoral communities. Land and herds were divided among the emperor, the Sun, and the peasants. Farmers used hoes, digging sticks, and tecllas (foot plows) with a point of hard wood or bronze. Where steep slopes made farming difficult, a remedy was found by making terraces.

Terrace culture was adopted by the Incas on a massive scale. They carried fertile topsoil up the mountain from the valley below, then laid it on a gravel base. Stone walls kept the earth in place, and stone irrigation channels brought water over long distances. Terraces were narrow on steep hillsides, but became wider lower down. By this method, the Incas increased the area of land available, and prevented erosion of the soil.

At high altitudes, people tended llama and alpaca herds. They also cultivated quinoa (a cereal), and potatoes. Corn was grown in warm valleys and on low-lying slopes. In the hotter lowlands, products included cotton, avocados, tomatoes, squash, chili peppers, beans, peanuts, honey, and various fruits.

▲ High in the Bolivian Andes, in the city of La Paz, this woman sells some of the many varieties of potatoes that are still grown in the region.

Animal Farming

Crucial to the Andean way of life were the camelids: llama, alpaca, vicuña, and guanaco. The guanaco and vicuña roamed freely. But llama and alpaca herds were tended by full-time shepherds. The quality of fleeces was graded; vicuña wool was used to weave the finest clothing.

The hunting of game was strictly regulated by Inca laws, but the domesticated guinea pig served in most households as a regular source of meat. Guinea pigs lived in the home and were fed on green plants and food scraps.

◀ The corn cob shown here was cast in silver by Inca metalsmiths. Corn was eaten in everyday life and was used to make *chicha* (a kind of beer).

Within the Inca empire, highland farmers cultivated more than 200 varieties of potatoes at altitudes of up to 16,400 ft. (5,000 m). This frost-resistant root crop, domesticated locally over thousands of years, required neither irrigation nor fertilizers. After four years of cultivation, land was left to lie fallow for seven years. Slow-ripening, bitter varieties of potatos were repeatedly exposed to frost and sun, then pressed into a food called Chuño.

Living Standards and State Control

Agricultural communities were viewed as units of production, and every aspect of life was regulated by government officials. Homes were visited by inspectors, who checked up on hygiene and living standards. Houses belonging to members of a large family were grouped around a shared compound. Inca rural dwellings were usually rectangular. Often built from stone with thatched roofs, they were virtually unfurnished and contained few possessions. Ornamentation was forbidden. Food was prepared in clay pots on a clay hearth at the center of the house. The clothing permitted by the state was simple and uniform: no modifications were allowed. Brides and grooms were allowed two outfits in llama wool, one for holidays and one for work.

▶ Many ancient customs are still practiced in the Andes. Like their ancestors, families who live on the shores of Lake Titicaca use reeds to make lightweight fishing boats. The couple seen here are drying their fish in the sun.

◀ On the fourth day after birth, a baby was put into a wooden cradle and tied in. Cradles had legs: usually, one leg was shorter than the others so that the cradle could be rocked. For its first three months of life, the baby was tightly wrapped in swaddling clothes. It was rarely embraced.

The Cycle of Life

Births were welcomed, because children would be able to help their families when they grew up. Infants lay in wooden cradles; when they were old enough to crawl, they played in a pit in the ground. At the age of one or two, they were named during a special hair-cutting ceremony. Garcilaso de la Vega described the upbringing given to all Inca children. There was little pampering: infants were washed in cold water and often exposed to the night air and dew.

The sons of peasants received no formal education. By helping their parents, they acquired the practical skills needed for adult life. When he reached puberty, a boy received his first loincloth in a simple celebration.

Inca healers understood the virtues of plants. Sprains and sore joints were covered with the heated leaves of a shrub; a type of bark, boiled in water, was applied to wounds. Coca leaves were used to calm the symptoms of hunger, tiredness, and pain and to combat the effects of altitude sickness in the high Andes. Surgery was sometimes practiced in Tahuantinsuyu.

Young girls, if chosen, were sent away to the Acllahuasi. The remainder married local youths, with the permission of the Curaca. Weddings were marked by feasting and drinking. Although men of noble rank could take second wives, this was rarely permitted to commoners.

A high value was attached to hard work. Households were obliged to help each other with difficult tasks such as house building or plowing. Harsh punishments were given to those who upset the social balance. Adulterers and murderers were tortured or put to death. Thieves were forced to work on plantations in the hotlands. Those who showed a lack of respect for the emperor or the state were imprisoned.

Religious festivities provided a welcome release from the drudgery of everyday life. People paid their respects to local divinities, venerated their dead ancestors, and celebrated the agricultural cycle with music, dancing, and feasting.

49

CHAPTER 8

The Spanish Conquest and After

Civil War

Because Inca society was organized in the manner of a pyramid, too much power was held by the emperor at the very top: this was the empire's weakness. In 1525 Huayna Capac died without naming his successor. A quarrel broke out between his two sons, Atahuallpa and Huascar; civil war followed, and the empire began to break up.

Francisco Pizarro

In Europe, Spain was entering a period of increasing power. Francisco Pizarro was a Spanish soldier who had been abandoned as a child and could not read or write. Inspired by tales of distant lands, he set sail for the New World. In his first two expeditions to Peru he explored the northwest coast of South America. On his third, in 1532, he reached Tahuantinsuyu with 62 horsemen and 198 soldiers.

The Death of Atahuallpa

According to contemporary accounts, the Incas were awestruck by the appearance of the bearded Spaniards, armed with steel weapons and gunpowder, and mounted on horseback. Huascar's followers believed that Viracocha, their god, had sent the Spaniards on a divine mission to drive out Atahuallpa. Taking advantage of the civil war between the followers of Atahuallpa and Huascar, Pizarro played one group against another.

Atahuallpa was taken prisoner by Pizarro. Hoping to regain his freedom, Atahuallpa ordered his men to fill his prison with gold. After a mock trial, the Inca was put to death. This signaled the beginning of the end of the Inca empire. Pizarro was later assassinated by his fellow Spaniards. In 1536 the Incas staged an unsuccessful revolt against their new European rulers. The last Inca outpost, in the Urubamba Valley, held out until 1572. But most of Tahuantinsuyu became the Viceroyalty of Peru, and remained so until 1824.

◀ The Spanish conquerors were hungry for riches. Few objects made from precious metals escaped the Spaniards' melting pots. Fortunately, this gold pectoral (breastplate) from Colombia survived.

As the Spaniards rode up to meet Atahuallpa for the first time, the Inca was sitting among his noblemen, who were dressed in their finery. The Inca court made a very impressive sight. Atahuallpa had never before seen horses, and one of the Spanish soldiers noticed that he was obviously very interested in them. To impress Atahuallpa, the soldier put on a display of horsemanship. He galloped away, wheeled the horse around, reared up, and finally rode straight at Atahuallpa at full speed. He stopped just a few inches away from the Inca leader. Atahuallpa sat still —totally expressionless—and showed no fear at all. Atahuallpa's incredible bravery, along with the size and obvious discipline of the Inca soldiers, made the Spanish fearful of the Incas. Pizarro later convinced his men that the only way to gain power over the Incas was to capture Atahuallpa: without him to lead them, the Inca people would not offer much resistance. The following day, they put this daring plan into action. When Atahuallpa visited Pizarro's camp at Cajamarca, he was seized and held prisoner.

The Collapse of Inca Civilization

The Spanish Conquest was marked by many acts of savage cruelty. Throughout most of the land, destruction and misery reigned. The Inca system of agriculture and terracing declined: lands once productive became barren. Virtual slaves, the Amerindians—people who are native to the Americas—were worked to exhaustion by Spanish settlers. In the mines, large numbers died digging for silver and gold. Driven by their hunger for riches, the conquerors melted down virtually every object of precious metal. Even the Coricancha, admired for its splendor by Spanish observers, was stripped of its treasures: 700 loads of gold were removed from the House of the Sun.

Under Spanish rule the Inca system of knotting and "reading" quipus was lost forever. Although a small number of quipus survive in museums, we are unable to decode the information that they carry. Pedro de Cieza de León, a witness to the early years of conquest, praised the "truth and accuracy" of quipus. He wrote sadly: "It is no small sorrow to reflect that those Incas, even though they were heathens and idolaters, knew how to keep such good order… and that we Christians have destroyed so many kingdoms."

The Spanish Conquest caused countless deaths among the inhabitants of the New World. Weakened by overwork in mines and on plantations, Amerindians were vulnerable to diseases from Europe. Throughout Tahuantinsuyu, vast numbers died of smallpox, measles, whooping cough, and other infections. The smallpox virus spread rapidly south from Central America. According to some estimates, the native population of Peru dropped from some 32 million in 1520 to only 5 million by 1548.

Felipe Guamán Poma de Ayala

The downfall of the Inca empire is usually described from a Spanish perspective, but a unique record of sixteenth-century Inca life survives. Its author, Felipe Guamán Poma de Ayala, was a native Andean. Angered and saddened by the sufferings of his people, he traveled the length and breadth of his ravaged country, recording vanishing traditions and describing the horrors of the conquest. The resulting manuscript of 1,188 pages included 398 drawings, some of which are reproduced in this book.

Guamán Poma dedicated his exceptional work to the Spanish king, asking him for "the welfare, increase, and protection of the Indians of this realm." He asked the Spaniards: "[Why] do you wish to run the lives of foreigners when you cannot run your own? Why do you demand from the poorest man his mule, but never ask if he needs any help?" Guamán Poma's manuscript never reached the king. Instead it arrived in northern Europe and was eventually discovered in 1908 in the Royal Library in Copenhagen, Denmark.

▲ People in Europe were filled with curiosity about the inhabitants of the New World. They also wanted to know about the plants and animals. Pictures like this one showed the way of life of the Amerindians in a semitropical South American landscape.

▶ Using the architectural styles of Spain, Spanish settlers built towns and cities throughout their newly conquered territories. Cathedrals and churches, like this one in Lima, Peru, dominated the new urban landscape.

The Catholic Church

The Spanish conquerors came in search of gold, but they also spread the teachings of the Christian faith. In their desire to win souls, crusading friars tried to banish "pagan" beliefs. Idols were destroyed, and religious rituals were banned. The royal mummies were taken to Lima for a Christian burial. One witness described how the Incas knelt and sobbed as the mummies were carried past them out of Cuzco.

Using stones from Inca temples, the Spaniards built churches and cathedrals. In the heart of Cuzco, the mighty walls of the Coricancha became part of the Church of Santo Domingo. Almost all aspects of traditional culture were criticized as "backward" and "undesirable."

The End of Colonial Rule

For nearly 300 years, Spain controlled the lands that had once belonged to the Incas. Some surviving members of the Inca nobility came to terms with their conquerors and lived in comfort. Because Spanish men outnumbered Spanish women, many took Inca wives: their children, of mixed parentage, were known as Mestizos. Most Amerindians suffered under Spanish rule, however.

During the eighteenth century, more than a hundred rebellions broke out in different parts of Peru.

◀ This map of modern South America shows the countries that once made up the Inca empire. After independence from Spain, local wars caused a number of boundary changes. In the War of the Pacific, which began in 1879, Peru and Bolivia were defeated by Chile, and Peru lost its southernmost lands.

Simón Bolívar is a national hero in South America, where he is known as The Liberator. Born in 1783 in Venezuela, he helped to end Spain's colonial domination throughout the region.

South American independence was finally secured with the help of an Argentine general, a Venezuelan general, and Simón Bolívar, a Venezuelan soldier-statesman. Freed from Spanish rule, the lands of the old Inca empire were divided up into the republics of Peru, Bolivia (named in honor of Bolívar), Ecuador, and Chile. Throughout much of the nineteenth century, these new states fought against one another.

This photograph looks across a valley to the Peruvian town of Urubamba. Situated at 9,393 ft. (2,863 m), the town is surrounded by mountains. The Incas thought this valley was special: it is still known as the Sacred Valley. This was the site of the last Inca outpost, which held out against Spanish domination until 1572.

The Spanish Conquest of the Inca empire inspired many legends about lost cities and treasures. "El Dorado," which means "the Golden Man," came to symbolize fabulous wealth. The name "El Dorado" was originally given by sixteenth-century Spaniards to a semilegendary chieftain in the Colombian highlands, who anointed himself once a year with oil and gold dust. Then stories began to circulate, describing El Dorado as a city of gold. El Dorado became a magnet for treasure seekers during the colonial period.

CHAPTER 9

The Inca Legacy

Into the Twentieth Century

Peru, once the heartland of Tahuantinsuyu, is the third largest country in South America. It is populated by approximately 21 million people. Nearly half are Amerindians, descendants of the country's original inhabitants. Although Spanish is the dominant language, it has absorbed many Quechua words. Lima, the Peruvian capital, was founded by Pizarro in 1535. It was devastated by an earthquake in 1746 and badly damaged in 1970. Today, Lima is home to 7 million people, many of whom live in shanty settlements. Once described as the most beautiful city in the Spanish Americas, modern Lima has few old buildings. Foreign tourists who flock to Peru each year are drawn instead to Cuzco. Rebuilt after the conquest by Spanish settlers, the center of Cuzco is still characterized by its powerful Inca architecture.

Bolivia, straddling the Andes, was absorbed into Tahuantinsuyu. Long before the rise of the Incas, however, the builders of Tiahuanaco had dominated the Titicaca region. Today Bolivia has a population of about 7 million people. Of these, some 70 percent are Amerindians.

▶ In recent years archaeologists have made important finds at ancient sites such as Sipán, where royal tombs have yielded marvelous works of art. In this photograph, workmen are excavating the ruins of Chan Chan.

▼ On the coast of Peru, where the civilization of Nazca once flourished, mummified bodies and ancient artifacts have remained hidden for hundreds of years beneath the desert sands.

The relics of the past attract archaeologists, but they also attract looters. In international galleries and salerooms, a high value is placed on pre-conquest works of art. Looters are constantly on the lookout for tombs and other ancient sites. In Peru and Bolivia, as in Mexico or Guatemala, thieves ruthlessly plunder the remains of pre-conquest cultures.

Discovering the Past

For most of this century, archaeologists have been hard at work, trying to learn more about the Incas and their predecessors. New discoveries are constantly being made. Few have been as exciting, however, as that of Machu Picchu, the best preserved of all Inca towns. After the Spanish Conquest, it lay forgotten until 1911. Buried in forest, Machu Picchu was "discovered" at last by Hiram Bingham, an American explorer from Yale University.

With each passing decade, we learn more about the past. Museums throughout Peru and Bolivia reflect the pride that is now taken in the textiles, pottery, and surviving goldwork from Inca and other cultures.

Continuity with the Inca Past

Nearly five centuries after the Spanish Conquest, native inhabitants of the remote highlands still keep many of their traditions. Quechua, the language of the Inca empire, is today spoken by more than 12 million mountain dwellers. Other native languages have also survived: Aymara is widely used in the area around Lake Titicaca.

Continuity with the past is shown in many ways. In farming and pastoral communities, members of extended families still help one another with agricultural tasks. Herders still rear llama and alpaca in the grasslands. Farmers still grow ancient crops such as corn and potatoes. In Inca and pre-Inca times, people used bundles of dried reeds to construct lightweight boats. Today, at Titicaca, fishermen use long poles to propel reed boats with pointed bows across the waters of the lake, just as their ancestors used to do.

Inevitably, rural life has seen some changes. Many Andeans now sow nonnative cereals such as wheat and barley. Sometimes they breed sheep, cows, and other animals introduced from Spain. Andeans also travel on crowded buses and trucks. This mixture of the old and the new occurs in crafts such as weaving: although some garments are still woven on back-strap looms, others are produced on European-style treadle looms and finished with factory-made trimmings.

▶ This photograph shows a Peruvian market in Chinchero, which means "Village of the Rainbow." Wearing their distinctive clothing, Quechua-speaking women buy and sell a range of locally grown grain, potatoes, and other vegetables, as well as factory-made goods from outside the region.

▲ A boat of dried reeds being used on Lake Titicaca. In the background is a much larger boat, which has room for several passengers. Reed boats like these were used in Inca and pre-Inca times.

During the eighteenth century, the Incas mounted several revolts against Spanish rule. In an attempt to control its rebellious subjects, Spain imposed a law forbidding the wearing of native dress: Amerindians were required to adopt Spanish peasant clothing. Today men and women combine garments of European origin with traditionally woven bags, sashes, shawls, and ponchos.

During bustling Sunday markets and regional fairs, traders sell livestock, fruit and grain, hats and clothing, cooking pots, and herbs for curing. They also offer radios, cosmetics, patent medicines, and other articles from the "modern" world.

Europe continues to derive many benefits from the New World. Important medicines have come from the forests of the Amazon. Foodstuffs such as potatoes are crucial to our way of life: although we eat them almost daily, we forget that potatoes came to us originally from the civilizations of the Andes. In cities such as London and New York, the finest cloth is made from alpaca wool. Some imports are less welcome, however. Coca generates huge fortunes for cocaine barons who control sales of this illegal drug in Europe and in the United States.

Fiesta!

Festivals, which often last for several days, are an important part of community life. In many Quechua-speaking villages, professional craftspeople make elaborate dance masks and colorful costumes for performers. Musicians play ancient instruments such as the quena, as well as newly introduced brass instruments and the harp. Masses are celebrated by the Catholic clergy, and hundreds of firecrackers are shot off. The Feast of Corpus Christi, introduced by the Church as a substitute for Inti Raymi, is a great religious occasion.

In addition to community-based fiestas, there are important pilgrimages. One place of pilgrimage, Qoyllur Rit'i, lies on a remote and uninhabited mountain at 15,400 ft. (4,700 m). Before the conquest, Qoyllur Rit'i was venerated as a sacred site. Each year it is visited by the faithful, who flock by the thousands to pay their respects to the overwhelming powers of nature. During the ceremony, pilgrims form giant human lines in view of the surrounding peaks. From a high glacier, a block of ice is carried down: for the believers waiting below, the ice symbolizes not just water but also life itself. In Peru and Bolivia, rituals such as these draw deeply on ancient beliefs and customs. Despite centuries of oppression and poverty, the Inca heart still beats.

▼ After the conquest, Spanish missionaries banned Inti Raymi, the Inca festival of the Sun. Now, as this photograph shows, it has been revived. It is performed each year at Sacsahuaman, just outside Cuzco. The costumes of the performers give onlookers an idea of the splendor of the Incas' civilization.

Time Line

B.C.

17,600–12,700 Cave occupation in Ayacucho, Peru.

9000–5000 Bands of hunters in the High Andes.

5000 First experiments with farming on coast and in highlands.

900 Beginning of Chavín culture.

700 Beginning of the Paracas culture.

200 Chavín culture comes to an end.

A.D.

1 Beginning of Moche culture.

100 Tiahuanaco culture starts to flourish.

200 Paracas culture coming to an end. Nazca culture begins to flourish.

600 Nazca culture comes to an end.

700 Moche culture comes to an end.

900 Beginning of Chimú culture.

1100 Cuzco founded by the legendary Manco Capac, first Sapa Inca.

1250 Tiahuanaco culture ends.

1438 Yupanqui is proclaimed ninth Sapa Inca and takes the name of Pachacuti.

1450 Pachacuti enlarges the Inca empire through a series of local wars.

1470 The Incas conquer the Chimú.

1471 Topa Inca, the tenth Sapa Inca, embarks on an era of road building.

1492 Inca conquest of Chile.

1498 Huayna Capac, the eleventh Sapa Inca, extends the empire beyond Quito into Colombia.

1525 Huayna Capac dies. Civil war follows.

1532 Francisco Pizarro captures Atahuallpa.

1533 Atahuallpa is executed by the Spaniards.

1535 Collapse of the Inca empire.

1537 A Neo-Inca state is established at Vilcabamba.

1572 End of Neo-Inca state.

1780 Túpac Amaru II leads an unsuccessful uprising and is executed.

1824 After a decisive battle, independence is won from Spain for the republic of Peru.

1825 Independence is won for Bolivia, named after Simón Bolívar.

1879 Start of the War of the Pacific: Peru and Bolivia later defeated by Chile.

1911 Hiram Bingham discovers the Inca city of Machu Picchu.

Glossary

Acllas Young girls who lived in convents and were taught religious duties by the Mamacunas. Some Acllas became Virgins of the Sun.

Acllahuasi House of the Chosen Women and Guardian Mothers.

Adobe Unfired mud brick, dried in the sun.

Alpaca Domesticated camelid.

Amauta Wise man, teacher, adviser.

Amerindians Word used to describe the original inhabitants of the Americas and their descendants.

Ayllu Family or community group. Members of the Inca royal family belonged to royal ayllus. In a rural context, ayllus were agrarian communities linked by family ties.

Aymara A language and a people. The Aymara language is today spoken by many people near Lake Titicaca.

Camelid Belonging to the *Camelidae* family: includes the domesticated llama and alpaca as well as the wild guanaco and vicuña.

Coca Low-growing tropical bush. Leaves are chewed as a stimulant to banish hunger and exhaustion; they also combat altitude sickness.

Coricancha Literally, "Enclosure of Gold." This was the name of the House of the Sun, principal temple of the Inca religion in Cuzco. Provincial capitals had similar temples.

Coya Title given to the principal wife of the Inca emperor.

Curaca Non-Inca leader of subdued regions of the Inca empire.

Cuzco The Inca capital.

Equinox Time at which the sun crosses the equator: day and night are equal in length.

Fiesta Festival.

Guanaco Wild camelid.

Huaca Shrines, places, or objects regarded as sacred by the Incas and their subjects.

Llama Domesticated camelid.

Mamacunas Guardian Mothers who lived in convents and served the Inca religion.

Mestizo Person of mixed European and Amerindian descent.

Mit'a Public works tax paid by Inca subjects.

Oracle Person or thing serving as an infallible guide to those seeking advice and prophecy.

Plaza Open square in a town.

Quechua Term applied to a people, a language, and a province. The Quechua language was the official language of the Inca empire; today, it is spoken by about 12 million people from Ecuador to northern Argentina. Quechua is also the name of the Andean province where this language originated.

Quipu Knotted cord used by the Incas for recording information.

Sapa Inca The supreme Inca; (literally, "Unique Inca").

Shaman Non-Christian priest-doctor who may go into trancelike states and have divine visions.

Solstice The times—one in the winter and one in the summer—when the sun is farthest from the equator. When this turning point is reached, the sun appears to pause.

Tahuantinsuyu Inca empire: "Land of the Four Quarters." At its center was Cuzco.

Vicuña Wild camelid.

Yachahuasi House of Teaching.

Further Reading

Baquedano, Elizabeth. *Aztec, Inca, & Maya* (Eyewitness). New York: Knopf Books for Young Readers, 1993.

Brown, Dale ed. *Incas: Lords of Gold and Glory* (Lost Civilizations). New York: Hill and Wang, 1992.

Chrisp, Peter. *The Incas* (Look Into the Past). Austin, TX: Thomson Learning, 1994.

Kendall, Sarita. *The Incas* (Worlds of the Past). Parsippany, NJ: Silver Burdett Press, 1992.

Newman, Shirley P. *The Incas* (First Books). Danbury, CT: Franklin Watts, 1992.

Wood, Tim. *The Incas* (See Through History). New York: Viking Children's, 1996.

Index

Figures in bold are illustrations.